CULTURE in the Kitchen

FOODS OF Mexico

By Kevin Pearce

Gareth Stevens
Publishing

Please visit our website, www.garethstevens.com. For a free color catalog of all our high-quality books, call toll free 1-800-542-2595 or fax 1-877-542-2596.

Library of Congress Cataloging-in-Publication Data

Pearce, Kevin.
Foods of Mexico / Kevin Pearce.
    p. cm. — (Culture in the kitchen)
Includes index.
ISBN 978-1-4339-5716-1 (pbk.)
ISBN 978-1-4339-5717-8 (6-pack)
ISBN 978-1-4339-5714-7 (library binding)
1. Cooking, Mexican—Juvenile literature. 2. Food habits—Mexico—Juvenile literature. 3. Mexico—Social life and customs—Juvenile literature. I. Title.
TX716.M4P43 2011
641.5972—dc22

                                            2010050703

First Edition

Published in 2012 by
Gareth Stevens Publishing
111 East 14th Street, Suite 349
New York, NY 10003

Designer: Daniel Hosek
Editor: Therese Shea

Photo credits: Cover and all interior images Shutterstock.com.

Printed in the United States of America

CPSIA compliance information: Batch #CS11GS: For further information contact Gareth Stevens, New York, New York at 1-800-542-2595.

Contents

Mexico's Gift of Food 4

Three Important Foods 6

More Mexican Foods. 8

Corn Makes the Meal 10

Beans and Chocolate! 12

Local Foods 14

Unusual Foods. 16

Drinks of Mexico .18

Sweet Mexican Treats 20

Recipe: Salsa. 21

Glossary 22

For More Information. 23

Index 24

Words in the glossary appear in **bold** type the first time they are used in the text.

Mexico's Gift of Food

Mexico shares a border with the United States. As Mexicans and Americans traveled back and forth across that border, a love of Mexican food and **culture** grew in the United States. However, many foods in Mexican American restaurants are different from the foods that most Mexicans eat. For example, nachos aren't often seen in Mexico. They're "Tex-Mex," or a mix of Texan and Mexican **cuisines**. However, salsa is an **authentic** food of Mexico. Let's get a taste of more authentic Mexican foods!

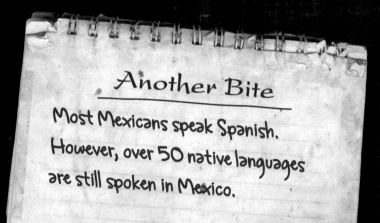

Another Bite

Most Mexicans speak Spanish. However, over 50 native languages are still spoken in Mexico.

Mexico has mountains, forests, beaches, and deserts. Mexicans have learned to use plants that grow in all of these settings for food. ▼

Canada

United States of America

Mexico

Three Important Foods

Three foods have always been an important part of Mexican cuisine. These are corn, squash, and beans. These crops were grown by native peoples in Mexico before the Spanish arrived in 1517.

Corn is the main **ingredient** in the flat, round bread called a tortilla. Tortillas are cooked on a hot grill or stove. Sometimes, they're eaten alongside a main dish. Other times, they're filled with food, folded or rolled, and eaten as the main dish. Tortillas are one food served everywhere in Mexico.

Another Bite

Rice became another important food of Mexico after the Spanish arrived. It's often served with beans.

Though tortillas can also be made with wheat flour, corn tortillas are still more popular in Mexico.

More Mexican Foods

Other native Mexican foods still grown today are tomatoes, sweet potatoes, and peppers. Hot chili peppers are ground into spicy sauces, or salsas. Avocados are often mashed into the dish called guacamole. Yellow fruits called papayas and green fruits called tomatillos are also found throughout Mexico.

chili peppers

tomatillos

The Spanish brought livestock, including cattle, pigs, and chickens. However, dairy foods and meat became just a small part of most Mexicans' meals. The Spanish also brought wheat, **lentils**, and onions.

Another Bite

Spain ruled Mexico for 300 years. The Spanish culture greatly affected Mexican cuisine.

Most salsas in Mexico are a mixture of tomatoes, peppers, and onions. Garlic and a bit of lime juice are sometimes added.

▼

Corn Makes the Meal

Corn tortillas are so popular in Mexico that they're sold by **street vendors**. Tacos, burritos, and quesadillas have become a popular part of US cuisine. In all of these, tortillas are filled with foods such as meat, beans, vegetables, and cheese. Enchiladas are tortillas dipped in chili sauce. *Enchilada* means "with chili."

Corn is important for tamales, too. In this dish, thick cornmeal paste covers a filling of meat and peppers. Then the tamales are wrapped in cornhusks and steamed. Corn is also boiled to make pozole, a thick stew.

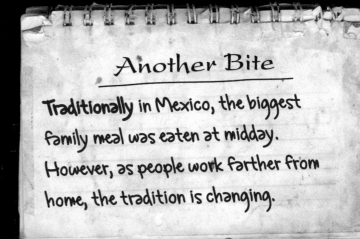

Another Bite

Traditionally in Mexico, the biggest family meal was eaten at midday. However, as people work farther from home, the tradition is changing.

quesadilla

burritos

◀ In a dish called huevos rancheros, fried eggs are served on top of a tortilla. The Spanish word for "eggs" is *huevos*.

11

Beans and Chocolate!

Other Mexican dishes don't use corn or tortillas. Sopa de lima is chicken soup with lime juice. The Spanish word for "soup" is *sopa*, and the word for "lime" is *lima*.

Beans, or *frijoles*, are served with many dishes. Pinto beans are often used in northern Mexico, while black beans are popular in southern Mexico.

Can you imagine having chocolate for dinner? Mole poblano is a sauce made from chocolate and peppers. It's spicy, not sweet like candy. It's usually poured over chicken.

Another Bite

Here are Spanish words for some kinds of foods: carnes (meats), pescados (fish), legumbres (vegetables), frutas (fruits), bebidas (drinks), and dulces (sweets).

◀ Hundreds of years ago, Mexicans used chocolate to make a drink for kings. Today it's used in sauces.

13

Local Foods

Northern Mexico was the birthplace of barbacoa, a method of steaming meat over coals in a pit. The word "barbecue" comes from this cooking style.

The Baja California **peninsula** in northwest Mexico is where fish tacos became famous. Some say that Caesar salad was first made here, too.

In southern Mexico, chicken is more common than beef. **Plantains** are also a popular food there. They can be boiled, baked, or fried.

plantain

The Yucatán peninsula is in southeast Mexico. Mayan Indians shaped the cuisine, which includes hard-boiled eggs and turkey.

A plentiful supply of fish makes fish tacos a common meal in Baja California. The area borders the Pacific Ocean and the Gulf of California.

Unusual Foods

All cultures have foods that seem unusual to others. Mexico is no different. In desert areas, prickly pear cactuses grow vegetables called nopals that are eaten raw or cooked. Octopus and squid are popular dishes in coastal areas. In central Mexico, the eggs of black ants are boiled and eaten in tortillas. **Fungus** is grown on corn and served in quesadillas and soups. In southern Mexico, grasshoppers are fried, spiced, and eaten as snacks. The meat of lizards called iguanas is eaten there as well.

The pink fruit on this prickly pear cactus, called tunas, must be carefully peeled before eating so that no spines remain.

17

Drinks of Mexico

A spicy Mexican meal needs to be followed by a cool drink. Mexicans have many cold, sweet drinks. Agua de jamaica is a deep red or purple drink made from flowers. Horchata is a sweet drink that uses ground rice or melon seeds. Fruit juices in Mexico include watermelon and orange juice.

A hot drink called atole—a mix of corn or rice meal, water, and spices—is prepared for holidays, such as Christmas and the Day of the Dead.

Another Bite

During Día de los Muertos (Day of the Dead), families remember their loved ones who have died. Special foods are eaten, such as skull-shaped candies and sweet breads.

This horchata is made with tiger nuts, which grow on the roots of the chufa sedge plant. Tiger nuts taste like almonds.

atole

19

Sweet Mexican Treats

Mexicans love sweet foods, too. Chocolate has been a part of Mexican cuisine for hundreds of years. Sweet breads and cookies are also favorites. In cities, street vendors roll around selling paletas, which are frozen treats made from cream or fruit juice.

Cajeta is sweetened milk that is heated until it tastes like caramel. Sometimes called dulce de leche, it's then poured over cake or ice cream. Mexican cuisine has something for everyone!

Flan is a sweet mix of eggs, milk, sugar, and vanilla.

Recipe:
Salsa
(requires the help of an adult)

Ingredients:

2 cups chopped tomatoes (6 or 7 tomatoes)

a bunch of fresh cilantro, chopped

6 cloves fresh garlic, chopped

1/2 onion, chopped

1 chili pepper, chopped

1/2 teaspoon salt

1 tablespoon lime juice

Directions:

Mix all ingredients well. Refrigerate overnight. Serve with tortilla chips.

Glossary

authentic: made the same way as the original

cuisine: a style of cooking

culture: the beliefs and ways of life of a group of people

fungus: a living thing that is somewhat like a plant, but doesn't make its own food, have leaves, or have a green color. Fungi include molds and mushrooms.

ingredient: a part of a mixture

lentil: a seed from a plant in the pea family that can be eaten

peninsula: a narrow piece of land that extends into water from the mainland

plantain: a greenish-yellow fruit that looks like a banana

street vendor: one who sells goods from a cart or stand on a street

traditionally: in a manner following past actions or ways of life

For More Information

Books

Streissguth, Thomas. *Mexico*. Minneapolis, MN: Lerner Publishing, 2008.

Ward, Karen. *Fun with Mexican Cooking*. New York, NY: PowerKids Press, 2010.

Websites

Mexican Cooking
www.kids-cooking-activities.com/Mexican-cooking.html
Try more recipes while reading facts about Mexico.

Mexican Kitchen Vocabulary
www.mexonline.com/mexfood.htm
Learn some Spanish words for common foods used in a Mexican kitchen.

Index

agua de jamaica 18
atole 18, 19
avocados 8
barbacoa 14
beans 6, 10, 12
black ant eggs 16
burritos 10, 11
cajeta 20
cheese 10
chicken 8, 12, 14
chocolate 12, 13, 20
cilantro 21
corn 6, 7, 10, 12, 16, 18
drinks 12, 13, 18
dulce de leche 20
enchiladas 10
fish 12, 14, 15
flan 20
fruit 8, 12, 17, 18, 20
fungus 16

garlic 9, 21
grasshoppers 16
guacamole 8
horchata 18, 19
huevos rancheros 11
iguanas 16
lime 9, 12, 21
meat 8, 10, 12, 14, 16
mole poblano 12
nopals 16
octopus 16
onions 8, 9, 21
paletas 20
papayas 8
peppers 8, 9, 10, 12, 21
plantains 14
pozole 10
prickly pear cactus 16, 17
quesadillas 10, 11, 16

rice 6, 18
salsa 4, 8, 9, 21
sopa de lima 12
squash 6
squid 16
sweet potatoes 8
sweets 12, 18, 20
tacos 10, 14, 15
tamales 10
tomatillos 8
tomatoes 8, 9, 21
tortillas 6, 7, 10, 11, 12, 16, 21
vegetables 10, 12, 16